con

C000144234

Hardware

Software   13 - 22

Networks and the Internet   23 - 33

WHAT IS I.C.T. ?

It is important to remember that I.C.T. is not only about computers.
Below are just some examples of items that fall under the I.C.T. banner.

INFORMATION

DVD Player

Television

Internet

Calculator

Radio

COMMUNICATION

e-mail

Telephone/Fax

Mobile phone

Data projector

Webcam

TECHNOLOGY

Digital camera

Laptop

Games console

Robots/roamers

MP3 players

daydream
Tel: 0800 060 0232
www.daydreameducation.co.uk

A COMPUTER SYSTEM

All the different parts of a computer, including the devices you plug into it, are known collectively as 'A Computer System'.

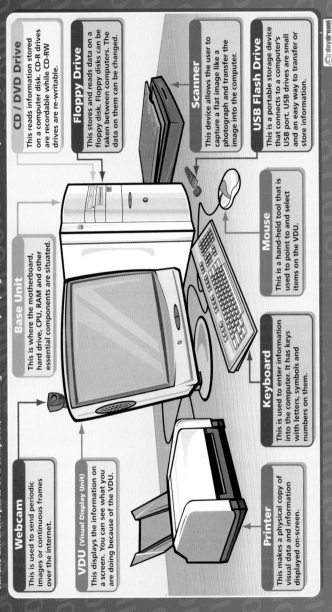

Webcam

This is used to send periodic images or continuous frames over the internet.

VDU (Visual Display Unit)

This displays the information on a screen. You can see what you are doing because of the VDU.

Base Unit

This is where the motherboard, hard drive, CPU, RAM and other essential components are situated.

CD / DVD Drive

This reads information stored on a computer disk. CD-R drives are recordable while CD-RW drives are re-writable.

Floppy Drive

This stores and reads data on a floppy disk. Floppy disks can be taken between computers. The data on them can be changed.

Scanner

This device allows the user to capture a flat image like a photograph and transfer the image into the computer.

USB Flash Drive

This is a portable storage device that connects to a computer's USB port. USB drives are small and an easy way to transfer or store information.

Mouse

This is a hand-held tool that is used to point to and select items on the VDU.

Keyboard

This is used to enter information into the computer. It has keys with letters, symbols and numbers on them.

Printer

This makes a physical copy of visual data and information displayed on-screen.

daydream

COMPUTER JARGON

Don't know your ROMs from your RAMs?
The language and terms used in computing can sometimes be
confusing. Here are some useful terms and explanations.

CD-ROM / DVD		• A CD-ROM is a compact disk that can store information, data, music, images etc. • A CD-R or CD-RW drive allows you to record data onto a disk. • A DVD is similar but it can store lots more data.
FLOPPY DISK		• A small portable plastic disk. • It holds very little data and is most commonly used for transferring small files such as text or Word documents.
HARD DISK		• A high-capacity storage drive. • The hard disk is usually internal and can store large programs along with personal files and documents.
CPU / PROCESSOR		• The Central Processing Unit (CPU) is a chip that powers the PC. • Its speed is measured in Megahertz (Mhz) and it determines how fast programs run.
ROM & RAM		• ROM (Read Only Memory) stores the instructions that tell the computer how to start working. • RAM (Random Access Memory) stores data while the computer is running but loses it when it is switched off.
MOTHER-BOARD		• The motherboard is the main circuit board inside your PC, It connects the CPU, RAM, disk drives and graphics / sound cards.
Gb / Mb		• Gigabytes (Gb) and Megabytes (Mb) are measurements of storage space. • A Gb is equal to a thousand Mb.
PORT		• A slot or plug, usually on the rear of a PC unit, that allows you to plug in external devices such as printers, scanners, cameras etc. to the PC.
PERIPHERAL		• Describes any item that can be attached to a PC but is not essential, such as a printer, scanner, camera etc.
MONITOR / VDU		• The Visual Display Unit (VDU) is the screen on which information and images can be viewed. • Laptops and modern monitors have a thinner VDU that is known as an LCD (Liquid Crystal Display).
VIRUS		• A virus is a program that spreads over a network or via e-mail. • Viruses are created deliberately to annoy or to destroy data.
NETWORK		• A Network links computers together so they can exchange information. • A user can send information such as text or graphics to another computer on the same network.

visit **www.daydreameducation.co.uk** for more information

WHAT GOES WHERE?

Because so many different things can be plugged into a PC,
it is sometimes difficult to know what goes where.

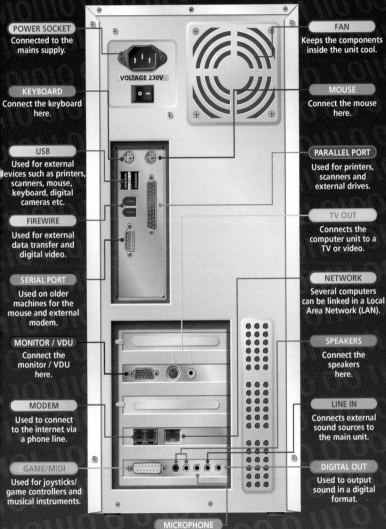

POWER SOCKET
Connected to the mains supply.

VOLTAGE 230V

KEYBOARD
Connect the keyboard here.

USB
Used for external devices such as printers, scanners, mouse, keyboard, digital cameras etc.

FIREWIRE
Used for external data transfer and digital video.

SERIAL PORT
Used on older machines for the mouse and external modem.

MONITOR / VDU
Connect the monitor / VDU here.

MODEM
Used to connect to the internet via a phone line.

GAME/MIDI
Used for joysticks/ game controllers and musical instruments.

FAN
Keeps the components inside the unit cool.

MOUSE
Connect the mouse here.

PARALLEL PORT
Used for printers, scanners and external drives.

TV OUT
Connects the computer unit to a TV or video.

NETWORK
Several computers can be linked in a Local Area Network (LAN).

SPEAKERS
Connect the speakers here.

LINE IN
Connects external sound sources to the main unit.

DIGITAL OUT
Used to output sound in a digital format.

MICROPHONE
Allows speech recognition.

daydream education

INPUT

Input is the information the user puts into the computer. To do this the user needs input devices. Input devices are used to capture data that the user inputs into the computer.

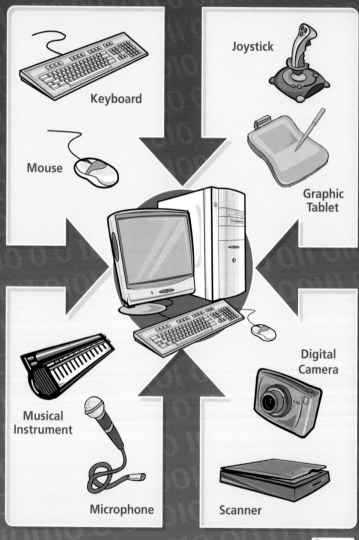

Keyboard

Joystick

Mouse

Graphic Tablet

Musical Instrument

Digital Camera

Microphone

Scanner

OUTPUT

Output is the data you receive after completing a process (word-processing etc.).
Output devices pass data back to the user from a completed process.

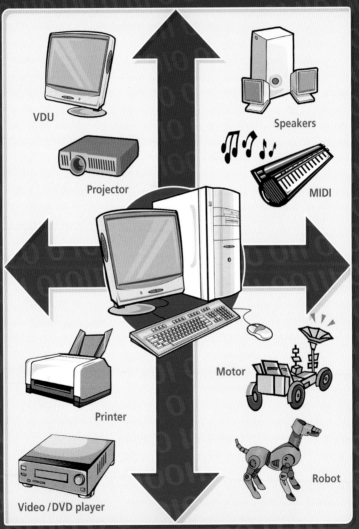

VDU

Speakers

Projector

MIDI

Printer

Motor

Video / DVD player

Robot

STORING DATA

Data can be stored on **internal storage** or **external storage** devices. Internal storage devices are inside your computer's processing unit. External storage devices are separate from your computer.

HARD DISKS

- Most hard disks are built into your computer and store data internally.
- Hard disks hold a large amount of data including your operating system and programs.
- Data on a hard disk can be accessed quickly.

OPTICAL DISKS

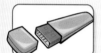

- Optical disks are external storage devices with very high capacity.
- The most common type is the CD-ROM which is used for multimedia software.
- DVDs can store an even larger amount of data, so a film can fit onto one disk.

USB DRIVES

- USB drives are portable storage devices that connect to a computer's USB port.
- They are a small and easy way to transfer or store information.

MAGNETIC TAPES

- Although tapes can hold a large amount of data you cannot randomly access data and transfer is very slow.
- Magnetic tapes are usually external devices, normally used for backup.

FLOPPY DISKS

- Floppy disks are external storage devices that are made of magnetised plastic.
- Floppy disks hold a relatively small amount of data and are often used as backup or to transfer data between computers.

daydream

TEL 0800 000 0000
www.daydreameducation.co.uk

visit **www.daydreameducation.co.uk** for more information

USING A KEYBOARD

A computer keyboard has many keys to help you operate the computer. Below are some important keys.

Tab Key
This key allows you to move along a line to a predetermined place.

Function Keys
Quick access to common functions within certain applications.

Back Space
Use this key to delete the letter before the cursor.

Enter (Return)
This key is pressed to start a new line or paragraph or to enter a piece of information.

Number Keypad
This is an extra set of numbers which is easier to use when you have lots of numbers to type.

Shift Key
You press this to access symbols that are above others on a key. You also use it when you want a single letter to be Upper Case (Capital). There are two shift keys on the keyboard.

Cursor Keys
These keys have arrow directions on them. You use them to move around text.

Space Bar
This allows you to insert blank spaces within text.

Caps Lock
This key locks the capitals so that all the letters typed are in UPPER CASE.

HEALTH AND SAFETY

As computers are used more and more, it is becoming apparent that regular users can suffer from health problems.

Common Problems

Visual Problems

Muscle & Posture Problems

R.S.I

REPETITIVE STRAIN INJURY

Symptoms:
- Some people suffer from aches and pains resulting from repeated activities such as using the mouse or typing.
- Possible joint damage can also occur.

Solutions:
- Use a wrist support along with an ergonomic keyboard.
- Forearms should be kept horizontal.

MUSCLE & POSTURE PROBLEMS

Symptoms:
- Bad posture or poorly-designed chairs can lead to back problems later in life.
- Sitting still for long periods of time can also lead to muscular strain and circulation problems.

Solutions:
- Take breaks and stretch your legs at regular intervals.
- Use only an ergonomically-designed chair.

VISUAL PROBLEMS

Symptoms:
- Spending too long looking at a monitor can lead to eye strain, headaches and discomfort.
- Bad lighting in an office can make reading a monitor difficult and put additional strain on the eyes.

Solutions:
- Make sure your eyes are level with the monitor.
- Good background lighting and a monitor filter reduce glare.

OPERATING SYSTEMS

The **Operating System (OS)** is the software that enables the application software and the rest of the computer system to work. Types of OS include Mac OS, DOS and Windows.

FIVE TASKS OF OPERATING SYSTEMS

1 **Manage System Resources**
e.g. allocating memory in the form of RAM to particular tasks.

2 **Communication between Software and Hardware**
e.g. clicking on the 'Print' icon will result in the printer printing.

3 **Monitor Performance**
e.g. providing error messages to the user (Disc not readable etc.).

4 **Operate Utilities**
e.g. starting virus scanning and diagnostic software.

5 **Operate Applications**
e.g. word processors - Microsoft Word running in Windows.

NETWORK OS

- The OS monitors the use of a network by different users.
- It monitors access time, system security and shared resources.
- Operating systems designed to run networks include Windows NT, UNIX and Linux.

MULTI-TASKING

- An OS can appear to run more than one program at a time.
- It doesn't happen at the same time - it is an illusion caused by the processor's (CPU's) speed.
- The CPU actually divides its time between tasks and completes parts in succession.

ICONS

Icons are small pictures which help us use computers.

Start

Internet	E-Mail	Local Disk	CD-ROM	Floppy Disk	Folder
Minimise	Maximise	Restore Down	Close	Log Off	Shut Down

APPLICATION

New	Save	Open	Print	Hyperlink	Table
Cut	Copy	Paste	Undo	Redo	Spell Check

INTERNET

Back	Forward	Stop	Refresh	Home	Search

GRAPHICS SOFTWARE

Graphics software is used to create or manipulate images.
Computer graphics usually come in two formats: Bitmapped and Vector.

USES

- To create drawings and diagrams.
- To manipulate existing images.
- For special effects for films.
- For animation.
- To create visuals for websites.

TOOLS

- Graphics programs use tools to create images.
- Tools are usually selected from an on-screen toolbox or palette.
- Tools include: zoom, colour swatches, paintbrushes, airbrushes, text, shapes and effects filters.

BITMAPS

- Images are represented as a sequence of dots called pixels.
- Each dot is stored separately and uses a lot of memory.
- Bitmapped files can be used in most programs.
- Image loses quality when enlarged.

VECTORS

- Images are stored as a sequence of instructions.
- Images can be reduced or enlarged without losing quality.
- Files do not use a lot of memory.
- Not all software is compatible with vector-based images.

SOFTWARE

Software is the term used to describe the programs that the computer runs.

INSTALLATION

Software can be installed in several ways:

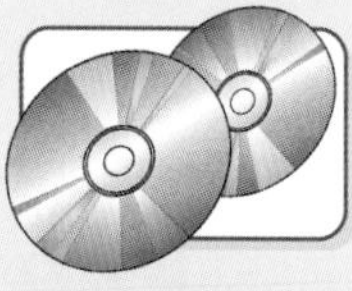

CD ROM / DVD

Floppy disk

Internet download

APPLICATIONS

Applications, or generic programs, are the programs most commonly used, such as:

Word-processors

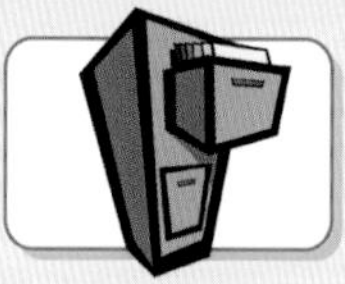

Databases

Graphic packages

Spreadsheets

Internet browsers

e-mail

Can you think of others?

OPERATING SYSTEMS

The Operating System (O.S.) allows the application software to run on the hardware.

WINDOWS® **MAC OS®** **UNIX®**

WORD-PROCESSING

A word-processing program assists you in writing letters, stories and many other kinds of text.
Below are some of the many features of a word-processing program.

TOOL BAR

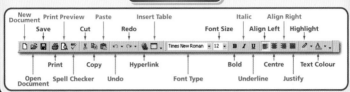

New Document | Print Preview | Paste | Insert Table | Italic | Align Right
Save | Cut | Redo | Font Size | Align Left | Highlight
Print | Copy | Hyperlink | Bold | Centre | Text Colour
Open Document | Spell Checker | Undo | Font Type | Underline | Justify

Spelling and Grammar

- Check your document for spelling errors.
- Caution should be taken as it only picks up words that are not in its dictionary.
- Words used incorrectly aren't always noticed.
- Check your grammar and look up words in a thesaurus.

LAYOUT

Edit and Amend

- Text can be deleted character by character or in highlighted blocks.
- Replacement text can be added at any point.
- Text or graphics can be cut or copied and pasted elsewhere.

Font Styles

- Font style (such as Arial, Times, Gill Sans etc.).
- Colour.
- Regular, **Bold**, *Italic*.
- Size, Size, Size.

Other features can be changed and customised for attractive presentation.

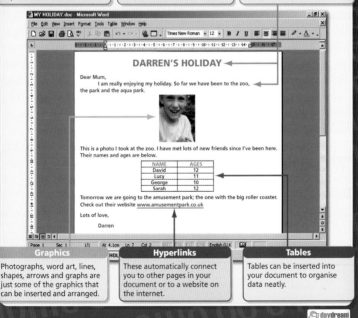

Graphics

Photographs, word art, lines, shapes, arrows and graphs are just some of the graphics that can be inserted and arranged.

Hyperlinks

These automatically connect you to other pages in your document or to a website on the internet.

Tables

Tables can be inserted into your document to organise data neatly.

DATABASES & SPREADSHEETS

DATABASES

Databases are organised collections of data stored on a computer.

Records
A record runs in rows and contains data in each field.

Fields
Fields run in columns. Each field is made up of related characters.

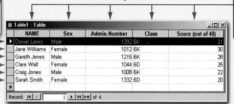

Table1 : Table				
NAME	**Sex**	**Admin. Number**	**Class**	**Score (out of 40)**
Daniel Lewis	Male	1392	6K	31
Jane Williams	Female	1012	6K	30
Gareth Jones	Male	1215	6K	28
Clare Wall	Female	1044	6D	25
Craig Jones	Male	1008	6K	22
Sarah Smith	Female	1332	6D	20

Record: 1 of 6

Databases
Databases allow the user to organise information in different ways (Table 1 is in order of scores and Table 2 in order of the 'Admin. Number').

Key Field
The Key Field is a field (in this case the admin. number) which makes each record unique.

Table2 : Table				
NAME	**Sex**	**Admin. Number**	**Class**	**Score (out of 40)**
Craig Jones	Male	1008	6K	22
Jane Williams	Female	1012	6K	30
Clare Wall	Female	1044	6D	25
Gareth Jones	Male	1215	6K	28
Sarah Smith	Female	1332	6D	20
Daniel Lewis	Male	1392	6K	31

Record: 6 of 6

Databases allow you to

 SORT
 SEARCH
 STORE
 DISPLAY

SPREADSHEETS

Spreadsheet software is used to perform calculations and to model situations.

Formula
- The user can create formulae within cells to work out calculations.
- The formula is shown for the selected cell.
- Once entered, formulae are hidden.
- As the scores are entered the cell is automatically updated.

Cell
Each cell in a spreadsheet has a coordinate e.g. 'F4' which can contain a formula, in this case: =AVERAGE(C4,D4,E4).

Microsoft Excel - Maths Results.xls
F4 = =AVERAGE(C4,D4,E4)

	NAME	SCORE TEST 1	SCORE TEST 2	SCORE TEST 3	AVERAGE
	David Williams	35	30	28	31.0
	Sarah Smith	28	20	24	24.0
	Craig Jones	26	21	31	26.0
	Jon Powell	27	31	29	29.0
	Gareth Jones	29	25	30	28.0
	Daniel Lewis	32	25		28.5

Rows
Rows go horizontally. This is row '8'.

Columns
Columns go vertically. This is column 'F'.

DATA LOGGING

Data logging is when information is captured and stored using sensors.
This information is then stored in the computer for analysis.

HARDWARE AND SOFTWARE

Input Sensor
This converts environmental signals (e.g. light or sound) into electrical energy that produces an analogue or digital signal.

Analogue Signals
Analogue signals are created when the sensor measures variables e.g. a range of temperatures.

Digital Signals
Digital signals are created when the sensor records single events e.g. cars going in and out of a car park.

Analogue to Digital
Analogue signals need to be converted to digital before they can be read by a computer.

WHAT IS MEASURED?

Light **Temperature** **Sound** **Pressure** **Air Pressure** **Infra-red Continuity** **Radio-activity**

BENEFITS

Hostile Environments
Data logging can record information in hostile, dangerous environments.

No Breaks
Data logging machines work until programmed not to. No need for breaks for sleeping and eating!

Accuracy
Intervals between measurements are more accurate than when done manually.

Time Scale
Data can be collected from something that happens very quickly or very slowly.

COMPUTER SIMULATIONS

Computer software allows us to model 'real life' situations in which we can test products or phenomena. Extreme examples of these are flight simulations and car-crash test systems.

SPREADSHEETS

- These can be used to model situations involving the use of formulae.

NAME	SCORE TEST 1	SCORE TEST 2	SCORE TEST 3	AVERAGE
David Williams	35	30	28	31.0
Sarah Smith	28	20	24	24.0
Craig Jones	26	21	31	26.0
Jon Powell	27	31	29	29.0
Gareth Jones	29	25	30	28.0
Daniel Lewis	32	25		28.5

- Spreadsheets can include variables. When they change, other data in the model change automatically.

C.A.D

- Computer-Aided Design (CAD) is used to create 2D and 3D graphical images.

- The images or models are based on data fed into the package by the user.

EXPERT SYSTEMS

- These simulate the knowledge of a human expert, containing data on specific subjects.

- The system asks the user questions, the answers to which lead to suggested solutions.

VIRTUAL REALITY

- VR models are extremely large and complex and give the user a realistic experience.

- This includes movement, sound and, with a special visor, realistic views.

ADVANTAGES

- Running a simulation is cheaper than the real thing.
- Models can be made to make useful predictions and prevent mistakes.
- Dangerous events can be studied in safety.

DISADVANTAGES

- A simulation is only as good as the program it's based on.
- Results can be misleading and present an inaccurate prediction.
- Setting up is often time consuming and expensive.

FILE EXTENSIONS

.tif

File extensions are the letters after the full stop at the end of a filename. They tell the computer what type of file it is.

.sys

COMMON EXTENSIONS

.exe	**Executable Program** Programs such as Word or Excel are executable files.	**.doc**	**Word Document** Used for Microsoft Word files.
.txt	**Plain Text** A basic form of text file.	**.xls**	**Excel Spreadsheet** Used for Microsoft Excel files.
.rtf	**Rich Text Format** A text file with more formatting options.	**.ppt**	**Powerpoint Presentation** Used for Microsoft Powerpoint files.
.html	**Hypertext Mark-up Language** Used for most webpages.	**.zip**	**Zip File** A file which has been compressed. (Takes up less room on the disk.)

MULTIMEDIA

Some of the more common image, video, and sound files are shown below.

.jpg	**Joint Photographic Experts Group** A graphic file with variable compression.	**.pdf**	**Portable Document Format** Used largely for on-screen versions of user manuals.
.gif	**Graphic Interchange Format** A graphic file used for websites.	**.avi**	**Audio Video Interleave** The most common Windows video file.
.tiff	**Tagged Image File Format** A higher-quality graphic file.	**.wav**	**Wave File** Windows sound file.
.bmp	**Bitmap** A Windows bitmap file.	**.mp3**	**MPEG-1, Audio Layer 3** A compressed sound file used on the web.

SYSTEM

These files should not be touched, as they help the computer function.

.bat	**Batch File** Used with MS Dos.	**.drv**	**Driver** Helps Windows talk to the hardware and peripherals.
.com	**Command** A Windows system file.	**.sys**	**System** A Windows system file.
.dll	**Dynamic Link Library** A Windows system file.	**.ini**	**Initiation** A Windows system file.

daydream
EDUCATION

TEL. 0000 000 0000
www.daydreameducation.co.uk

MULTIMEDIA PRESENTATIONS

Multimedia software is being used more and more to help people give professional-looking presentations.

HOW THEY HELP

- Presentations can be used to demonstrate a new idea or to communicate information.

- Software can be used to give a presentation with or without a speaker.

- Interactive whiteboards are commonly used in multimedia presentations.

- Pupils and teachers can present information in a colourful and varied way.

FEATURES

- Multimedia presentations usually consist of a series of slides that contain a number of frames including text, sound, images etc.

- Slides can be changed on a timer or manually through the computer.

- Graphs, spreadsheets and databases can also be inserted as frames within a slide.

- Text and images can be manipulated to appear on screen in an interesting way.

- Presentations can be printed slide by slide, or as a whole, or with additional notes as a handout.

- Presentations can also include animations, moving images and video.

COMPUTERS IN SOCIETY

Computers are being used increasingly in society and they affect our everyday lives.

IN SCHOOL

Computers are used in schools to help manage them efficiently and to improve the quality of teaching and learning.

- Attendance, tests and reports are recorded, marked and written electronically.
- PCs and the internet are used in the classroom.
- Teachers use computers to plan and prepare their lessons.
- Lessons may be presented on an interactive whiteboard.

AT WORK

Computers are used more and more in offices. The eventual goal is to have fully computerised offices.

- Many offices use intranet. This is a site-specific mini internet run using a company's own network.
- e-mails are commonly used instead of the more traditional memoranda.
- Multimedia presentations can be given.
- Teleconferencing means less need for business travel.

IN BANKS

In addition to the uses 'AT WORK', banks need computers to run multiple accounts.

- Clearing Houses use computers to process cheques.
- ATM's allow a person to access their account 24 hours a day and withdraw cash.
- Internet banking has become increasingly popular, allowing you to control your account via a PC.

IN SHOPS

Shops use computers to make shoppers' lives simpler and to manage stock easier.

- Shoppers can pay by cash, cheque or credit/debit card at tills.
- Bar Codes allow tills to recognise and price stock and re-order when stock is low.
- Loyalty cards are used to reward customers and identify their shopping habits.

WAYS TO COMMUNICATE

There are many ways in which people can communicate.
Here are some of the most popular ways.

 ADVANTAGES

DISADVANTAGES

POST

- Very little technology required
- Large items can be sent

- Slow
- Can be expensive

TELEPHONE

- People enjoy talking
- Immediate contact

- Limited business hours
- Expensive long distance

FAX

- Send words and pictures
- Hard copy provided

- Slow for large documents
- Junk faxes waste paper

E-MAIL

- Quick worldwide delivery
- Send files as attachments

- Internet access needed
- Not secure and risk of viruses

MOBILE PHONE

- Use practically anywhere
- Send text messages

- Needs regular recharging
- Worries about radiation

INTERNET

- Accessible world wide
- Wide range of information

- Service provider needed
- Can be hard to find information

VIDEO CONFERENCING

- Vision and sound
- Saves time and expenses

- Initially expensive
- Needs simultaneous meetings

SATELLITE

- Large amounts of data
- TV and business uses

- Expensive to launch
- Expensive to access

e-mail

e-mail is becoming increasingly popular as a method of communication. Here is a quick guide to using this useful tool.

CREATE THE MESSAGE

e-mails are usually text based. If using web-based e-mail, you need to connect prior to writing.

CONNECT TO THE INTERNET

This is done through a modem and telephone line, an ISDN or broadband connection. Your ISP will take you to your message centre.

ATTACHMENTS & SENDING

Enter the recipient's address and attach files (these can include pictures, graphs, music etc.). Confirm and send.

MESSAGE SENT

Your message will be sent almost instantly from your ISP (Internet Service Provider) to a mailbox at the recipient's ISP.

RECIPIENT READS MESSAGE

When the recipient next accesses their e-mail account, they will find a new message in their inbox. They then just download and read.

 100%   Data

 You've Got Mail!

When receiving an e-mail, click on the title and it will automatically download and appear on the screen. **Always be cautious of attachments** as they could contain viruses. Only open attachments when you are certain of their contents.

 100%   Data

 daydream

TEL 0800 000 0000
www.daydreameducation.co.uk

INTERNET FEATURES

Here are just some of the many important features of the internet.

WWW Internet

- All the web pages that exist on servers around the world are known collectively as the *Internet*.
- Web pages are used for **entertainment**, **advertising**, **business**, **information** and much much more!

Chat Rooms

- Using an applet in a browser, it is possible to have real-time text conversations with other logged-on users.

e-mail

- One of the most popular reasons for accessing the internet is to use an e-mail address.
- It's much quicker and cheaper to communicate via e-mail than by conventional mail.

File Transfer

- When you copy a file from one location to another it is known as a file transfer.
- A common example of this is downloading music from file-sharing sites.

e-commerce

- When a company sells its products online, this is known as e-commerce.
- Some companies only conduct business through the internet. Others have added it to their existing business to attract even more customers.
- Online supermarkets and banks have been a particular success.

News Groups

- People who have similar interests, or who want to debate an issue, can post comments on message boards for all members to read.

Education

- You can use the internet for interactive learning, to revise for exams, for research, to learn about new hobbies and much more.

Search Engines

- Search Engines are web sites that helps you search for other websites.
- They allow the user to perform searches based on a keyword.

INTERNET JARGON

Don't know your HTML from your URL?
The language and terms used on the internet can sometimes be
confusing. Here are some useful terms and explanations.

KBPS		• Kilobits per second - measurement of the modem speed. • This dictates how quickly internet pages can be opened and navigated.
BROWSER		• The software used to navigate the internet. • The most common browsers are Microsoft Internet Explorer and Netscape Navigator.
BOOKMARK		• Browsers often have a bookmark option. • Sometimes known as *Favourites* it allows you to store the addresses of your favourite websites for quick access.
SEARCH ENGINE		• A large website used to help find other websites on the web. • You type in a keyword and the search engine displays the most relevant websites.
WEBSITE		• A page or linked pages of information, images, sound etc. on the world wide web. • A website is identified by the www. prefix.
HOMEPAGE		• A website that automatically loads when you log on to the internet. • Your homepage is usually provided by your service provider but it can be customised to your needs.
FILE SERVER		• A central computer that holds files, programs and sites for other computers to access via a network such as the internet.
URL		• Uniform Resource Locator - the unique web address of a website. • Has www. prefix and relevant extension (.co.uk, .com, .org etc.) e.g. www.daydreameducation.co.uk
E-MAIL		• Electronic Mail - mainly text-based communication transferred via the web or network from computer to computer. • Additional files can be sent as attachments.
ISP		• Internet Service Provider - provides your software connection to the internet and the world wide web for a set fee. • BT and AOL are examples of ISPs.
HTML		• The code used to write web pages. • HTML often appears as an extension to a web address.
DOWNLOAD		• The process of copying a file from the web on to your PC. • The opposite of download is upload, to place a file on the web.

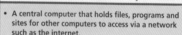

daydream
TEL 0800 000 8231
www.daydreameducation.co.uk

INTERNET ADVANTAGES

More and more people are using the internet.
Here are some of the advantages.

IT IS VAST!

A huge amount of material is available and it is still growing.

Large amounts
of data

School work
and research

Access to
expert knowledge

MULTIMEDIA

Ideas and messages can be put across in many imaginative and exciting ways.

Sounds

Images

Movie clips

EASILY UPDATED

Because of the simplicity of putting information on to web sites,
the latest information can be accessed almost instantly.

News

Sports results

Financial Information

EASY ACCESS

Most people in the developed world now have some form
of access to the information on the internet.

Through a mobile

At school or work

At home

INTERNET DISADVANTAGES

LOCATING INFORMATION

- Because of the large amount of material on the internet it can be difficult to find what you want.

Vague search engines

Too much information

SECURITY

- Most information on the internet is not secure and may be intercepted or hacked.

Credit card fraud

Personal details

UNDESIRABLE MATERIAL

- International laws governing the internet are often not compatible between countries.

Offensive material

Viruses

UNRELIABLE FILTERS

- Filters can be unreliable and can often prevent genuine and useful materials from being viewed.

Deny access to genuine material

Misleading information

FINDING A WEBSITE

The **Uniform Resource Locator** (URL) is the
address of a web page. All websites have a URL.

USING URLs

http://
Hypertext Transfer Protocol - the method that browsers use to read web pages.

www.
This stands for World Wide Web.

daydreameducation
Domain Name - usually the full or abbreviated name of the company/organisation.

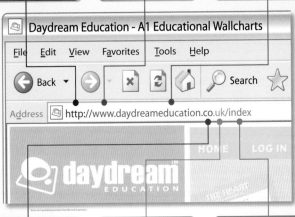

Daydream Education - A1 Educational Wallcharts

File   Edit   View   Favorites   Tools   Help

Back ▾   Search

Address   http://www.daydreameducation.co.uk/index

HOME   LOG IN

.co
Domain type. This is a company.

.uk
Country Code. This site is in the UK.

/index
This tells the computer exactly which page within the site you are looking for.

DOMAIN TYPES

.co - company (non-US)
.com - company
.ac - university, etc.
.org - organisation
.sch - school
.net - general
.gov - government

COUNTRY CODES

.uk - United Kingdom
.fr - France
.au - Australia
.nz - New Zealand
.de - Germany
.us - United States*

*Many U.S. websites use .com, .net or .org rather than .us.

REMEMBER!
URLs must be typed in accurately - right down to
full stops and correctly-placed slashes.

DESIGNING A WEBSITE

When designing a website, it is important to research and consider what makes a good website. Remember these five simple steps to ensuring an effective website.

1 THINK ABOUT USERS

- Before you begin, think about who your intended audience is.
- Test your initial ideas on typical target users, evaluate and improve.

2 KEEP LAYOUT CLEAR

- The layout should be clear and easy to follow.
- This should not change through the site as it could cause confusion.

3 SIMPLE DESIGN

- Text should be easy to read and contrasting with the background.
- This makes the site easier on the eye and will provide quality print outs.

4 MINIMISE GRAPHICS

- Graphics make download time slower and should be kept to a minimum.
- Most users will not wait more than a few seconds before giving up on a site.

5 SIMPLIFY HYPERLINKS

- Hyperlinks are essential for navigation but should be minimised to avoid complexity.
- A general rule would be to avoid more than four links to any destination in the site.

THE DATA PROTECTION ACT

- When using the internet, users are often required to provide personal information about themselves.

- Because many groups of people expressed concern about the use of data, the British government passed the **Data Protection Act**.

- Businesses that use data must register and comply with the Data Protection Act.

100% ▼ Data ▼

- Data must not be acquired and processed unless there is a lawful reason to do so.

- Data must be processed within the rights of the person supplying the data.

- Data must only be used for specific, lawful purposes.

- Personal data must be accurate and up-to-date.

- Provision must be made for the correction of data held.

- Suitable measures should be taken to ensure the safety of personal data.

- Data held should be the minimum required for the purpose and should not be kept longer than is reasonable.

- Data is not to be transferred to countries outside the European Economic area.

100% ▼ Data ▼

WHAT ARE NETWORKS?

Two or more computers joined together are known as a network. A network enables these computers to communicate with each other. There are two types of network: LAN and WAN.

LANs → LOCAL AREA NETWORKS

- LAN networks are the type that you find in most schools and small offices, when all the computers on one site are connected together.

- They require a network file server to run the software needed and to store files created by the users.

- Workstations (or terminals) are usually connected with cabling, allowing access to all software and files in the network. Radio links are also possible.

WANs → WIDE AREA NETWORKS

- WANs are used when the computers that need to be connected are in completely different places.

- They are connected using a modem via telephone and ISDN lines. Satellite or microwaves can be used at greater expense.

- WANs allow staff to access data whilst working away from their main work place.

- The Internet is an example of a WAN.

notes